Monographic Journals of the Near East *Afroasiatic Linguistics* 6/6 (September 1979)

THE IIwy VERBS AND THE VOWEL SYSTEM OF PROTO-WEST SEMITIC

by

A.M.R. Aristar
University of Chicago

Dissatisfaction is expressed with the theories generally offered as explanation for the development of the II*wy* verbs in West Semitic. As a result, recourse is made to an internal reconstruction of the relevant group as it occurs in Classical Arabic, in terms of its linguistic context in that language. From this the conclusion is drawn that mid vowels (*e:* and *o:*) existed as phonemes in these verbs at an earlier stage. The comparative data from Ethiopic and Hebrew is then examined, and found to be in broad agreement with the Arabic conclusions. Reasons for the loss of the phonemes, and the circumstances of that loss, are briefly discussed.

CONTENTS

1. INTRODUCTION

It is a simple fact that no adequate reconstruction of the linguistic history of the Semitic group of languages has been carried out. We do not lack diachronic studies of the group; but the majority of such efforts have proceeded from what are essentially a priori standpoints. The data has never been viewed on its own terms, and allowed to suggest a solution in terms of modern linguistic methodology.

Proto-Semitic or West Semitic reconstructions of the G perfect of the class of roots which have *w* or *y* as their second radical (henceforwards called the "II*wy* class") often contain the consonants *w* or *y*, i.e. Cl. Arabic *qa:ma* < **qawama* 'he stood up', *sa:ra* < **sayara* 'he went', etc. (cf. Cowan 1966). Since such segments do not appear in the cognates of this grammatical form in any of the relevant languages, the reconstruction can only be based on the model of the strong roots in Semitic, where a triconsonantal, and thus a three-syllabled, pattern appears, e.g. *kataba* 'he wrote'. The postulation of the missing segment as *w* or *y* is obviously due to the presence of such in other forms derived from the same roots, e.g. the Arabic verbal nouns *qawmatun*, *sayrun* etc., as well as in some of the derived stems of the verb, for example the D stem *qawwama* 'he set up'.

There is a serious methodological error here. The fact that the semi-vowels are found in some forms derived from the roots of the II*wy* class is evidence for their existence at some period in all forms of those roots. But it is decisively not evidence that they are to be reconstructed there for either Proto-Semitic or West Semitic. With regard to alternations, internal reconstruction cannot do more than indicate that a regularity earlier existed and what it is most likely to have been. Unless special conditions obtain, it cannot fix a stage at which the regularity is to be found. This comparative reconstruction can do, but only when one language has preserved a regularity in place of the alternation, or has an alternation which complements, but is not the same as, the other. If both have the same alternation, then it must be reconstructed for the proto-language as well, with the marginal proviso that parallel development is a possibility to be investigated. If all the languages of a large group have it, then parallel development is no longer a possibility which can reasonable be contemplated. This is the situation found for the II*wy* root-class as a whole in Semitic.

Thus, to reconstruct **qawama* is equivalent to internal reconstruction. This might in other circumstances be an innocuous error, but in the specific case of Semitic it has serious empirical consequences. For it denies us an explanation of the non-appearance of the trisyllable forms in any Semitic language, and it necessitates the redundant specification of the change for each and in terms of the phonology of each, which means that at best changes are being described which never took place. Whatever each language shows with regard to the bisyllabic forms is treated as idiosyncratic, and therefore ignored as explanation of the facts of other languages of the family. In short, internal reconstruction has been misused, and the results of this misuse have caused sound comparative reconstruction to be neglected.

Moreover, there is no really secure evidence that semi-vowels ever existed in the G form: in no case is alternation between *w* and *y* and lack of them found within a paradigm, and it is only in terms of a paradigm that internal reconstruction is really trustworthy. *w* and *y* appear rather as a distinguishing feature of a particular derived form, whether nominal or verbal. Therefore, the occurrence of the semi-vowel might well be the result of derivational processes of which we are no longer aware, especially since the II*wy* class is probably an old one.

---

[1] I would like to thank Dr. Robert Hetzron for the comments he made upon an earlier version of this paper. While we may not agree on the specific issues and questions involved, it was his observations which stimulated me to discuss many of them, and for this I am deeply grateful.

2. RECONSTRUCTION

One other reconstruction has been commonly proposed, the so-called biliteral reconstruction, where the first and third radicals are separated by a low vowel, either long or short, e.g. **qa:ma* or **qama*, **sa:ra*, etc. (Blake 1942). This, however, faces insuperable difficulties in at least three languages: Arabic, Hebrew, and Ethiopic.

In the Arabic reflexes of these verbs, the perfect of the G stem exhibits a curious alternation between a short, high vowel, either back or front, and a long, low vowel. In one class, composed of II*w* verbs, the first and second persons, as also the 3rd f. pl., have *u*, e.g. *dumtum* 'you m. pl. lasted' etc. In the other class, composed of both II*w* and II*y* verbs, these same persons have *i*, e.g. *sirtum* 'you m. pl. went'. All other persons, in both classes, have *a:*, e.g. *da:ma* 'he lasted', *sa:ra* 'he went'.

The biliteral theory has two problems here. Firstly, how is the derivation of *i* and *u* from **a* to be explained? Secondly, how does it explain the regular split of the posited phoneme? There is no conditioning factor whatsoever present, either at the surface or underlying; there is not even a correlation between root-class and the known reflexes. No analogical process could have thus produced the forms, for there is nothing to which the verbs could analogize. Unless therefore the forms are to be seen as totally unquantifiable, we can only now resort to rigorous internal reconstruction for a solution.

The only distinction in terms of phonological context between the long and short vowels forms lies in syllabic structure. Where *i* and *u* appear in closed syllables, *a:* appears in open ones. This distinction must then in some way be linked with the origin of the alternation, for suppletion is not here a possibility—all II*wy* verbs behave in this way. Syllabic structure is not likely to be the immediate cause of the varying vocalic qualities. Rather, specified syllabic patterns must be the input to a rule which affects vowels in some way.

Only one such rule is found in Arabic, a phonotactic constraint which shortens long vowels in closed syllables.[2] This is such a powerful rule that it even operates across word-boundaries, e.g. /kalba: mraʾatin/ → *kalba mraʾatin* 'a woman's two dogs'.

There is no other means of characterizing or explaining the Arabic alternation but in terms of this constraint. That alternation must then have had origin in an allophonic variation in quality between long and short vowels. Therefore *i* and *u* must, in the G perfect of the II*wy* class, be the reflexes of the short grades of two separate vowels which existed at an earlier stage of Arabic, and were qualitatively and phonemically distinct from /a:/, /u:/, and /i:/, for the short grades of these vowels do not differ in quality to the long, e.g. *yaxa:fu* 'he will be afraid', *yaxaf* 'let him be afraid', *yaqu:mu* 'he will stand', *yaqum* 'let him stand', *yasi:ru* 'he will go', *yasir* 'let him go'. Nor is there any discernible phonological differentiation in context between the II*wy* vowels and the others.

Since the II*wy* alternation is between the high front vowel *i* and the low vowel *a:* on the one hand, and the high back *u* against low *a:* on the other, the only feasible reconstructions are the mid vowels */e:/ in the first case and */o:/ in the second. By the syllabic

---

[2] This is an oversimplification of the rule but not in such a way as to affect the argument. Long vowels before geminated consonants in certain morphological forms, prominently the active participle, do not shorten. In all cases where this is found, the ablaut-pattern requires the presence of an additional short vowel, missing in the form in question, which would have opened the syllable containing the long vowel. The only way to account for this distribution is to accept that syncope of that short vowel has occurred and that the constraint formerly operated unrestrictedly, e.g. *ʿa:mmun* < **ʿa:mimun*. See Hetzron (1974).

structure constraint these would shorten to *e and *o in closed syllables, remaining long in open, e.g. *sirtu* < **sertu*, *sa:ra* < **se:ra*, and *qumtu* < **qomtu*, *qa:ma* < **qo:ma*.[3]

The phenomena known to the early Arabic grammarians as *ʾimāla* and *tafkhīm* are noteworthy in the light of the above reconstruction.

3. *IMĀLA* AND *TAFKHĪM*

3.1. DESCRIPTION

Jazārī states that *tafkhīm* was the opposite of *ʾimāla*; that is, it was a term used to denote long back vowels which were non-high. It had two realizations, *tafxi:mun mutawassiṭun* or 'middle *tafkhīm*' and *tafxi:mun šadi:dun* or 'strong *tafkhīm*'. The former was phonetic *a:* or some similar vowel, the latter "the kind of vowel heard in Khurasān", i.e. phonetic *o:*. This second type, he adds, occurred in IIIw roots, e.g. in nouns such as *ṣalo:tun* 'prayer', *ḥayo:tun* 'life', etc. (Rabin 1951:105). In such words, indeed, strange spellings are sporadically found in both religious and secular writings, where the script-sign for *w* is written to indicate the mid vowel. A dialectal distinction was in evidence: Ibn Manẓūr makes it clear that, in some speech-groups, *tafkhīm* also showed itself in IIw roots, and offers the example of *qo:ma* (Rabin 1951:106). Little further comment is found about this vowel, and the segment was apparently not regarded as being of great importance in linguistic description. The situation is quite different with regard to *ʾimāla*.

This term obviously denotes either a mid or low fronted vowel *e:*. Ibn Mālik in the *Tawḍīḥ* describes it as "your taking the *fatḥa* [i.e. /a/] towards the *kasra*," i.e. towards /i/, (Howell 1886IV:I:738). The grammarians attribute this to two causes: either the surface presence of *y* or *i*, or "by derivation"—that is, the presence of *y* in the abstract underlying root-consonant skeleton. In this latter case, it will obviously not be present on the surface, e.g. *rade:* 'destruction' (construct form), root √*rdy* (Howell 1886:IV:I:738ff).

It occurs for later Arabic *a:* in nine positions:

1. Wherever the grapheme called *ʾalif maqṣūra* (the script-sign for *y*) is written, as well as in forms derived from these by suffixation of the feminine marker -*(a)tun*, e.g. *alfate:* 'the young man', *alfate:tu* 'the young woman'.

2. Where the middle radical is underlying *y*, e.g. *be:ʿa*, 'he sold', root *bye*.

3. In IIw verbs where "the *ʿayn* is pronounced with *kasra*" (Howell 1886IV:I:750), that is, where the vowel *i* alternates in the perfect with *a:*, e.g. *xiftu* thus *xe:fa*.

4. Immediately preceding *y*, e.g. *be:yana* 'he differed'.

5. Immediately after *y*, e.g. *baye:nun* 'explanation'.

---

[3]The exact phonemic status of these mid vowels is problematic, if earlier they had only existed in IIwy verbs. There is a strong likelihood, however, that this is an illusion produced by morphological accident, in that only in this class is there an alternation which allows us to demarcate them. This problem will be solved only by a comparative study of the Semitic vowels, which is certainly well overdue in any event. Possible candidates for W.S. mid vowels would be such words as Arabic *ǰa:run* 'neighbor' (cf. Hebrew *ge:r*).

6. After two consonants, the first of which is *y*, provided *u* does not intervene, e.g. *baytahe:* 'her house' (acc.) but not **baytuhe:* (nom.).

7. Immediately before a consonant which is followed by *i*, e.g. *ᶜe:limun* 'wise'.

8. Following *i* and a consonant, e.g. *ᶜine:dun* 'obstinacy'.

9. Immediately after *e:*, e.g. *raᵓaytu ᶜime:de:* 'I saw a pillar', derived from *ᶜime:dan* (acc.), where by regular rule in Cl. Arabic, *-an* becomes *a:*, and is then imalized.

These can be divided into two groups by the action of the *mufakhkhamāt* upon them. These were the pharyngealized series of consonants, as well as the two velar fricatives, which blocked *ᵓimāla* in certain cases, but only when the segment which triggered the *ᵓimāla* was present at the surface in the same word (Howell 1886IV:I:738). Thus, in *γa:ᵓibun* 'absent' *a:* remained, while *ke:milun* (instead of *ka:milun*) 'perfect' showed *ᵓimāla*. But *xe:fa* and *baγe:* 'he wished' exhibit no effect from their mufakhkhama consonants. In modern terms, this clearly corresponds to a distinction characterizable in terms of the phoneme: only allophones were subject to the influence of these consonants.[4]

It is not necessarily true, however, that we are dealing with more than one fronting phenomenon. It might be possible to derive even phonemic *e:* from /a/ fronted adjacent to *y* or *i*, if loss of these segments could be demonstrated to have taken place at an earlier stage. In fact, the evidence for the loss not only of *y*, but also of *w*, is very strong.

3.2. LOSS OF *w* AND *y* IN ARABIC

Regular alternation within paradigms between the presence and absence of semi-vowels occurs in all III*wy* verbs and many nouns of this root-class. All such verbs which have a 3m.sg. perfect written with *ᵓalif maqṣūra* have a diphthong *ay* preceding inflectional suffixes which begin with a consonant. All those with ordinary *ᵓalif* have the diphthong *aw* before these suffixes. Thus one finds *bana:* 'he built' but *banaytu* 'I built'; and beside *ᶜada:* 'he ran' is found *ᶜadawtu* 'I ran'. In the case of the nouns, similar behavior is displayed. *ᵓAlif maqṣūra* in the singular marks that a dual with consonantal *y* will appear, e.g. *alfata:* 'the young man', *alfataya:ni* 'the two young men'. The others have *w* in the same position, *alᶜaṣa:* 'the stick', *alᶜaṣawa:ni* 'the two sticks'.

With such alternations it seems difficult to escape the conclusion that, at an earlier stage, the semi-vowels occurred in all forms of these words. There is even documentary evidence for this, for some tribes are recorded as using forms such as *fatayya* 'my young man', and *qafayya* 'my neck', which would be the regularly derived reflexes of **fatayiya* and **qafawiya* (Ibn ᶜAqil 1851:345). They are certainly not explicable by a resort to analogy, for there are no parallel forms which could serve as a model. And if the analogy is to be with triradicality itself, then no motivation for a distinction between the two classes is available. An arbitrary difference would have to be proposed which

---

[4]It is difficult to understand the logic of Cantineau (1960:96ff), who calls *ᵓimāla* an "unconditioned phenomenon". On the basis of the statements of the Arab grammarians, he tries to see all cases of *ᵓimāla* as being a result of assimilation either to surface *i* or *y* or to the underlying root-consonant *y*. Since, to take one example, the *ᵓimāla* found in words such as *me:ta* 'he died' cannot be accounted for in this way, he rejects all *ᵓimāla* as unconditioned. In short, on the basis of the data a hypothesis has been formed. This was then turned back upon the data, becoming the metric by which the very data upon which it was formed is rejected. And since *ᵓimāla* is thereby proved to be unconditioned, the hypothesis-metric is itself now rejected, for it has shown itself to be wrong!

would serve no purpose but to produce, ultimately, a different semi-vowel, yet it is only that difference which provides clear grounds for the demarcation of the two groups but which is nevertheless ignored because of an a priori assumption that the forms are to be derived from biradicals. In any event, the comparative evidence is difficult to reject: Ethiopic and South Arabic, the only languages to preserve a distinction unequivocally between two groups of III*wy* roots (it exists marginally in Ugaritic and Akkadian), show the reconstructible segments overtly. What is more, in those cases where a reflex of the same Semitic root is found in another Semitic language, the class into which they fall is generally the same—cf. Ethiopic *talawku* and *bakayku* with Arabic *talawtu* 'I followed' and *bakaytu* 'I wept'.

Obviously, *w* and *y* loss was not unconditional in Arabic. From the few examples given above a reasonable hypothesis would be that they fell everywhere except before long, low vowels, and before consonants, provided that *a* preceded.

If one searches for unisolated exceptions to this generalization, only two are visible: the energic forms of III*wy* verb-roots and one broken plural pattern.

Now, if the energic forms of the regular verb are compared to those of the III*wy* class, with imperfect vowel *a*, a strange fact emerges: the semi-vowel which appears bears no relation whatsoever to the root-class of a verb to which it belongs, which in this case is always III*y*. Instead, it is homorganic to a following high vowel, and *y* everywhere else, e.g. *tarḍayinna* 'you (f.sg.) will be satisfied' but *yarḍawunna* 'they (m.) will be satisfied'.

Given this situation, it is interesting to consider the fact that a unsophisticated synchronic analysis of this mood would state that it is formed by the affixation of various suffixes to the jussive mood: *-anna* to the 3rd sg., 1st sg. and 1st pl. as well as to the 2nd m.sg., e.g. *taktubanna* 'you (m.sg.) will write', *-inna* for the 2nd f.sg., e.g. *taktubinna* 'you (f.sg.) will write', and *-unna* for the 2nd and 3rd m.pl., e.g. *yaktubunna* 'they (m.) will write'. If the jussive forms of the III*wy* group have these suffixes added to them, the result is exactly the forms which do in fact occur, even including the anomalous semi-vowels, e.g. *yarḍaw* + *unna*, *tarḍay* + *inna* etc.

The energic, then, bears the signs of some morphological reformation. And it is difficult to see any cause which might have stimulated this except for the loss of semi-vowels, for, going by the analogy of the III*wy* noun-forms above, such a loss would have obliterated many of the person distinctions of the energic—a relatively rare mood and therefore not one likely to keep irregularities of such a sweeping kind—which in every other verb-class and mood had been preserved. For example, **tarḍanna* would have been derivable from the 2nd m.sg./3rd f.sg. **tarḍayanna*, 2nd f.sg. **tarḍayinna* and 2nd m.pl. **tarḍayunna*, while **yarḍanna* would have had origin in both 3rd m.sg. **yarḍayanna* and pl. **yarḍayunna*.

This is not proof of such a process. But what Ibn Mālik says in the *Tashīl* comes as close to it as one ever finds, for he states quite plainly that a general rule was applicable in some dialects: *y* drops if it occurs before the energic suffix and follows *a*, and he gives as example *tarḍanna* for the normal Cl. Arabic *tarḍayanna* (Rabin 1951: 199).

The other exception is the sequence *awa*, found in the broken plural pattern *faᶜalatun*, a common plural for the present participle, e.g. *xawanatun* 'traitors', *ḥawakatun*, etc. These might be taken as counter-evidence to *w*/*y* drop. In fact, they point to strong evidence for it. For in every case where such exists, a second form exhibiting *w*-loss is present as an allomorph, e.g. *xa:natun*, *ḥa:katun*, which is always the more common plural. Since these are found nowhere but in the II*w* class, they could scarcely have been formed by analogy. The *xawanatun* type, however, would easily be produced by analogy to the strong roots, many of which form such plurals, for broken plural formation is a living part of the morphology.

There is however one set of forms which forces revision of the earlier statement of the conditioning of *w/y* fall. Final diphthongs appear to have remained, e.g. *ᵓaw* 'or', *kay* 'so that', *bintay* 'two girls' (constr.), and these cannot be dismissed as neologisms. It seems therefore that diphthongs were preserved at a word-boundary, which means that only intervocalic *w* and *y* were lost after *a* and only inside words.

In the case of the verb-forms, then, **ᶜadawa* 'he ran' and **banaya* 'he built' can be reconstructed. In the noun-forms, since *w/y* must have preceded a vowel in order to fall, and the only vowels which could conceivably have appeared there are the case-vowels, **ᶜaṣaw{u/a/i}u* and **fatay{u/a/i}u* may be reconstructed.

Thus, it can be demonstrated quite conclusively that both *ᵓimāla* and *tafkhīm* can, in the case of the IIIwy verbs, be attributed to assimilation of *a* to an adjacent semi-vowel and that in many cases the triggering segment has been lost by phonological change.

But if this is so, we are forced to one conclusion: if the forms in question are derived from *w/y* loss, any other forms so derived should show the same or similar reflexes. This is not the case with the II*wy* verbs, for the short grades of the vowels produced by *w/y* fall are identical to those of long vowels which were not so derivable and which were never imalized or tafkhimīzed, e.g. *banat* 'she built' < **banayat*. Therefore the imalīzed and tafkhīmized vowels of the II*wy* class, with their high short-vowelled alternants, cannot have been produced by *w/y* fall unless such fall antedates the existence of the III*wy* class. And since the III*wy* class is reconstructible for Proto-West Semitic, semi-vowels could not have existed in the II*wy* class at that stage.

Even the inscriptional evidence from Arabia (Ṣafaitic, Thamudic and Liḥyanite) supports this interpretation, for all these show *w* and *y* regularly written for the III*wy* class of verbs (*w* less often than *y*) but very rarely for the II*wy*. The few cases which do occur must be regarded as either derived themes, where consonantal *w* or *y* would in some cases appear, or sporadic attempts at writing vowels (Caskel 1968; Harding 1952; Jamme 1967; van den Branden 1950).

The dialectal evidence enables the distinction between the two classes to be made even more overt.

3.3. *ᵓIMĀLA* AND *TAFKHĪM* IN THE DIALECTS

Sībawayhī writes that ᵓimāla is found, in all dialects, in III*wy* roots, both nominals and verbs, where a long non-high vowel is the final segment and is not part of a suffix. He goes on to say, on the same page, "*ᵓAlifs* [i.e. *a:*] are imalized in all II*w* or II*y* verbs, where the first radical of the perfect has *kasra* [i.e. *i* in such forms as *mittu* 'I died', *sirtu* 'I went']. One follows the example of the *kasra* as one follows the example of the *yāᵓ* written in place of the *ᵓalif* [e.g. *bana:* 'he built', written *bny*]. This is the speech of some Ḥijazīs. The majority do not (so) imalize."[5] (Sībawayhī 1975:4:120)

This is an ambiguous statement. He may be asserting either that only some Ḥijāzīs imalized II*wy* verbs, while all other Arabs did not, or that all other Arabs did, along with a few Ḥijāzīs.

---

[5]Standard edition pp. 280-81. In Arabic, *wa-mimma: yumi:lu:na ᵓalifahu kullu šayᵓin ka:na min bana:ti l-ya:ᵓi wa-l-wa:wi mimma: huma: fi:hi ᶜaynun, ᵓiδa: ka:na ᵓawwalu faᶜaltu maksu:ran. naħaw naħwa l-kasri kama: naħaw naħwa l-ya:ᵓi fi:ma: ka:nat ᵓalifuhu fi: mawdiᶜi l-ya:ᵓi, wa-hiya luγatun li-baᶜdi ᵓahli l-ħija:zi. fa-ᵓamma: l-ᶜa:mmatu fa-la: yumi:lu:na.*

Observe that different reciters are recorded as reading various verbs with *ʾimāla*. Ḥamza of Kūfa read six such verbs with strong *ʾimāla* (Cantineau 1960:99), probably phonetic *e:* or *ɛ:*, Nāfiʿ of Madīna read them with middle *ʾimāla* (phonetic *æ* ?). Ibn ʿAmīr read only two verbs in this way. Sībawayhī, later on the same page as his earlier statement, gives a number of examples of imalized verbs, *xe:fa* 'he feared', *ṭe:ba* 'it was good', *he:ba* 'he was afraid', without attributing them to any individual, and then adds specifically that he had heard the Ḥijāzī poet Kuthayyir-ʿAzzata say *se:ra* 'he became' and a Qur'ān-reader say *xe:fa*, both with *ʾimāla*, as if these utterances were unusual. This is a strange thing to do if this *ʾimāla* were an essentially Ḥijāzī process.

Farrāʿ's statement settles the question conclusively, as quoted by Ibn Yaʿīs: "The people of the Ḥijāz have *fatḥa* [i.e. *a*] in verbs such as *sa:ʾa*, *xa:fa*, *ja:ʾa* and *ka:da* [all of which have *a:* ~ *i* in the perfect] and in verbs mediae *wāw* and *yāʾ*. And the majority of the people of the Najd, namely Tamīn, ʾAsad, and Qays, incline towards *kasra* in the verbs mediae *y*, and in those mentioned, but *fatḥa* in verbs mediae *wāw* such as *qa:la* and *ja:la* [which have *a:* ~ *u* in the perfect]." (Rabin 1951:111-112)[6]

If these two authorities are taken together there is only one interpretation possible. Ḥijāzīs did not imalize II*wy* verbs while other groups, specifically the Eastern Arabs, did. Sībawayhī's statement cannot be taken any other way, unless one is also to take him as contradicting Farrāʿ.[7] And for this action there is no justification, especially when the totality of his comments are considered. We can now understand why he goes on to mention a Ḥijāzī poet as using a single form, and a Qur'ānic reader as using another. The Qur'ān was revealed in the Ḥijāzī dialect, and reciters were expected to conform to it.

It is thus also obvious why there is a constant citation by other writers of a small group of imalized verbs. These were atypical in Ḥijāzī dialect, and the aim of the discussion was clearly not to insert *ʾimāla* where readers might lack it but to ensure that they refrained from imalizing where the best reciters did not.

The same situation obtains with *tafkhīm*, though about this there is a great deal less discussion and no ambiguity. No commentator attributes the phenomenon to Ḥijāzī, and Jazārī plainly states that it was in fact not found in this speech-group except in III*wy* roots (Rabin 1951:105).

3.4. IMPLICATIONS

In II*wy* verbs then, both *ʾimāla* and *tafkhīm* were missing in the Ḥijāzi dialect, though they were present in II*wy* roots. The Qur'anic spellings support this, for while both are distinguished in III*wy* roots, from *a:*, and from each other (in the case of *o:* this is only sporadically done) there is never any such indication in the II*wy* forms in the standard text. This is not merely a matter of the position of the imalized vowel in the word, for when, by suffixation, an *e:* fell inside a word, the *yāʾ* was in earlier times still written, e.g. *rmyh* = *rame:hu* 'he threw it'[8] (Wright 1898:I:11).

There are thus two points to be made. Firstly, *ʾimāla* and *tafkhīm* can no longer be dismissed as allophonic phenomena in all cases, an action which in any event always rested

---

[6] I translate *yasru:na ʾila:* as 'incline towards'.

[7] As Rabin (1951:111-112) does.

[8] The *wāw* and *yāʾ* found written in III*wy* roots are probably relics from the time when these semi-vowels actually existed in the forms in question. After they fell, the two script-signs were reinterpreted as matres lectionis for the new phonemes /e:/, /o:/, and /ü:/.

upon insecure grounds (Cantineau 1960:96ff). As far as the II*wy* verbs are concerned, both phones appear in exactly the position which internal reconstruction would predict, i.e. *sirtu* thus *se:ra*, *qumtu* thus *qo:ma*. To reject *e:* and *o:* in such third person forms is in no way qualitatively different to saying that the short vowels *i* and *u* are, in a synchronic grammar of Classical Arabic, allophonic as well, and this is an obvious absurdity. The fact that some of the imalized verbs are of the II*w* class (*me:ta* 'he died', and *xe:fa* 'he feared', for example) is substantial evidence for the validity of the reconstruction. In these verbs *ʾimāla* cannot synchronically or diachronically be due to any segment *y*, and it is to the loss or "analogy"[9] of such a semi-vowel, along with surface *i*, that *ʾimāla* has been ascribed.

Secondly, it is in the very group which has been reconstructed as having */e:/ and */o:/, i.e. the II*wy* group, that mid vowels are lacking in the Ḥijāzī dialect. And this is strong evidence for their existence prior to that of the similar phones found in the III*wy* root-class. If these latter had existed as phonemes in Ḥijāzī concurrently with */e:/ and */o:/, it is difficult to see why one group should have been lost and the other preserved, for, by the evidence of the grammarians given above, they were indeed phonemic in some positions, e.g. *ʿane:* 'he meant', *ʿano:* 'he was humble', *ʿanne:* 'he tormented'-*ʿanna:* 'from us'.[10] The II*wy* mid vowels cannot have been produced later in non-Hijāzī dialects by some linguistic change, for there can scarcely exist a process which will split an earlier **ra:ma* meaning both 'he desired' and 'he went away' into **ro:ma* with the first meaning and **re:ma* with the second.[11] The only alternative to this would be to assert that *w* and *y* remained in the II*wy* G stem until or later than their loss in the III*wy* verbs, and this is simply not in conformity with the facts, either inscriptional or linguistic.

It would therefore seem that the short grades of two earlier Arabic phonemes */e:/ and */o:/ merged in all dialects with /i/ and /u/ respectively. The long grades were lost in Ḥijāzī before the rise of mid vowels as phonemes (though not necessarily as allophones) from other sources, but in Eastern Arabic the two groupings fell together into /e:/ and /o:/, before these in turn merged later with /a:/.

---

[9] The term analogy is used so loosely in Semitic linguistics as to become little more than a meaningless escape-route where complicated or obscure processes are involved. One does not deny its existence as a powerful force in linguistic change, especially in paradigm-regularization; but it should be the last, not the first, resort, for otherwise many valid generalizations will remain undiscovered.

[10] The grammarians' evidence as to the presence of *ʾimāla* and *tafkhīm* in the III*wy* group has, like that of its presence in the II*wy* group, been sometimes rejected as not being in conformity with reality, though why they should have invented such a synchronically odd distribution, let alone institute a spelling distinction between their inventions and other /a:/, is left unexplained. The justification often given for this rejection is that *ʾimāla* was also found, in some speech-groups, in the III*w* verb-class where *tafkhīm* was to be expected, although this was regarded as incorrect usage. But it is a historical fact that the III*y* group was suffering merger into the III*w*, and it is therefore scarcely surprising that *e:* should have begun to appear in both groups.

[11] Observe that the presence of mid vowels in such verbs is based on internal reconstruction as well, not merely the evidence of the grammarians.

4. THE COMPARATIVE EVIDENCE

4.1. ETHIOPIC

In Ethiopic, mid vowels are found throughout the perfect of the G stem, e.g. *k'omku* 'I stood up', *k'omä* 'he stood up', *šemku* 'I placed', *šemä* 'he placed'. Length is no longer phonemic in this language. This tense has, up to the present, been usually regarded as showing analogical extension of *e* and *o* from the third person, where **šayma* > *šemä* and **k'awma* > *k'omä*, into the first and second person, for a word-medial doubly closed syllable such as **k'awmku* is not an admissible structure in Ethiopic (or for that matter in any early Semitic language). Resort to analogy is always suspect, but in addition the third person forms which are supposed to have produced the mid vowels are impossible. The diphthongs there proposed cannot have existed in West Semitic, for Arabic has no such, and yet has preserved all diphthongs. The Ethiopic forms then would have to be derived from ones with intervocalic *w* and *y*, e.g. **k'awama* and **šayama* etc. and then syncope of the second vowel. Such syncope is required nowhere else in the language, and the rule is therefore ad hoc. The forms in question cannot be derived directly from the hypothetical **k'awama* and **šayama*, for intervocalic semi-vowels are elsewhere preserved, e.g. *täläwä* 'he followed' and *bäkäyä* 'he wept'.

It might be suggested that perhaps these triliteral forms are incorrect and that in fact those which gave rise to the Ethiopic mid vowels were instead of the pattern **k'awuma* or **šayira*, etc. Under such circumstances, loss of the second vowels could take place under one of two conditions: either because of assimilation of the high vowels to the preceding semi-vowel—because of their basic phonetic similarity this is not an unreasonable process—or as a result of the well-substantiated Ethiopic merger of **u* and **i* in *ə*, and its subsequent loss. After either of these, the changes *aw* > *o* and *ay* > *e* could take place normally. The mid vowels then spread into the **k'awama* and **šayara* patterns by analogy.

Observe that such an explanation is of no use in explaining the Arabic forms, for, as was discussed above, forms such as **ʿaṣawun* 'stick' (nom.) and **fatayin* 'young man' (gen.) must be reconstructed, and these have reflexes which are quite unlike those of the II*wy* verbs. Nor is it of any value in understanding the Hebrew reflexes, since **qawma* would have produced either **qawɛm* or **qo:m*, and neither of these occur. Even in the case of Ethiopic the problem of explaining in a non-ad hoc fashion how it was that the language could have allowed at an earlier stage a syllabic structure (i.e. **k'awmku*) which at both an earlier and a later stage it did not allow, would remain. The alternative to this would be to use again the concept of analogy from the third person into the first and second in order to derive the required forms.

But just as problematical as this is that the theory presupposes that the *faʿila* and *faʿula* patterns were either more common than the *faʿala* type or contained more common verbs. And this can hardly have been the case, for the *faʿila* pattern has an *a*-theme imperfect *ya/ifʿal(u)*, and by the evidence of all languages but Arabic—and even here examples are found (Wright 1896:I:59)—so did *faʿula*. This, in the case of II*wy* verbs, would produce imperfects **yaqa:mu*, **yasa:ru*, etc. Such imperfects do in fact occur, in Hebrew (*ye:ḇo:š* < **yiba:šu* 'he will be ashamed'), in Ethiopic (*yəbaʾ* 'let him come'), and in Arabic (*yaxa:fu* 'he will fear'), but they are extremely uncommon. In every case only one or two examples occur. And it does not seem possible that *faʿu/ila* could be powerful enough to oust the regular *faʿala* pattern in II*wy* verbs (in strong verbs the opposite has been the tendency in all languages) and then have the regular *u*- and *i*-theme imperfects *yafʿu/il(u)* have the opposite effect on their imperfects by in turn ousting the *a*-theme imperfects.

Obviously, a derivation of the Ethiopic forms from the biliteral reconstructions would require a change which is as ad hoc as the triliteral. It would, in fact, serve no other purpose but to produce the Ethiopic forms from the reconstructions proposed, for West

Semitic **a* or **a:* does not regularly become either *e* or *o*, nor is there any conditioning factor which could split the posited proto-phoneme.

4.2. HEBREW

Similar problems are found in Hebrew. It has never been adequately explained why forms such as *qa:m* 'he stood up' exist in the language, for if they are derived from West Semitic forms with the same long vowel, there is no reason why *a:* should not have become *o:* as other stressed **a:* did, e.g. *qo:ṭe:l*<**qa:ṭilu* 'killer'. An attempt to circumvent the difficulty by reconstructing **qawama*, etc. as existing at the time of the change will solve nothing. With such a form we are unable to account for the Canaanite *nu-uḫ-ti* 'I rested' (Böhl 1909:68) found in the Amarna letters instead of the **na-aḫ-ti* which Hebrew *naḥti:* would have led us to expect. Moreover, if intervocalic *w* and *y* fell, a long vowel would result, which, in closed syllables, would be shortened and therefore could not take part in the change of stressed *a:* to *o:*, e.g. **qawamti* > **qa:mti* ⇢ **qamti*. An alternating paradigm should have been left, *qamti:* but **qo:m*, and this is nowhere found. And since 3rd persons are by far the most common, in spoken or written language, analogy from the 1st and 2nd persons into the 3rd is difficult to accept.

It has been asserted that Canaanite had indeed changed **qa:ma* to **qo:ma* (e.g. Bauer and Leander 1922:391) but that Hebrew then later brought back **qa:ma* from some unspecified speech-layer where it had remained. Disregarding the doubtful validity of this kind of explanation—it is neither verifiable nor falsifiable and is therefore equivalent to speculation—one can nevertheless not easily account in this way for the origin of *nu-uḫ-ti*, for it is still only in the 3rd person that long vowels would have remained. The Amarna form then, would have to be seen as an analogical extension of the mid vowel of the 3rd person into the 1st and 2nd (in cuneiform *u* is not distinguished from *o*). In any event, it is somewhat difficult to see why Hebrew should have replaced its own II*wy* verb-forms with items from the putative speech-layer yet left all the other cases of words with *o:* < **a:* unscathed, for there seems to be no reason why one morphological class should be singled out in this manner.

Birkeland (1940:42-50, 102-106) accepts the speech-mixture theory in its basics, but since he denies the existence of the vowel-shortening constraint in West Semitic and in Canaanite, he does not require analogy in order to derive the Amarna form from a posited **na:ḥti* for **a:* ⇢ *o:* here as well as in the 3rd person. Thus, *nu-uḫ-ti* is to be seen as the cuneiform rendition of **no:ḥti*, a form which was later replaced by the **na:ḥti* of the other speech-layer. This latter form is to be derived from a **qawama* which still existed in that speech-layer (as it did not in Amarna Canaanite) when **a:* ⇢ *o:*, for otherwise **qo:m* would be found.

The constraint, however, almost certainly did exist in central Semitic.[12] In Hebrew itself there is clear evidence for its operation, at a diachronically earlier stage. This language has jussive forms of the II*wy* verbs with short vowels, while the indicative has long, e.g. *ya:qom* 'let him stand', cf. *ya:qu:m* 'he will stand'. Such are inexplicable unless they are derived from earlier **yaqum* and **yaqu:mu*, which are identical to the Arabic, where the short vowels are an incidental result of the constraint. In order to derive the Hebrew forms from these reconstructs will require no more changes than would in any case be required to account for all the other words in the language. Observe too that Hebrew does in fact show short vowels in those syllables of the perfect which were closed before the fall of final short vowels.

[12]Though perhaps not in Proto-Semitic. The Akkadian data need analysis.

For this reason, Birkeland is compelled to assert that this language, internally, produced for itself the vowel-shortening constraint which earlier it was not supposed to have had. An exactly parallel innovation must be posited for Arabic and perhaps for Ethiopic, where such forms as *kʷən* are found, a common form for the imperative m.sg. 'be' (Dillmann 1907:182), which can only regularly be derived from an earlier **kun* ← **ku:n*. In open syllables *u*, the reflex of earlier **u:*, always appears, e.g. *kunu* 'be' m.pl.

Such explanations are patently of little value. Some other must clearly be sought, and one possibility does suggest itself.

The evidence shows that Phoenician, the closely-related sister-dialect of Hebrew, at one stage had four levels of vowel-height, three back vowels *u*, *o*, and ɔ in descending order, and the low vowel *a*, for in Phoenician **o* later merged in *u*, whereas ɔ did not, e.g. *ᶜu:lɔ:m* < **ᶜo:lɔ:m* 'eternity' (Harris 1939:44, 62). This did not take place in Hebrew. In both languages, though at different periods, all *a:* which existed at that point became ɔ:. In Hebrew, this happened after the Classical period, where *a:* is still found, e.g Classical *ᶜo:la:m*, later *ᶜo:lɔ:m*. The vowel *a:* did not merge with *o:*, which must have thus been a higher vowel than ɔ.

If Canaanite inherited a three height system of vowels, it is possible to account for these patterns and mergers as well as the forms displayed by the II*wy* verbs. If the West Semitic **o:* was at this time phonetically closer to ɔ:, the new incoming vowel would not merge with it but instead restrict its distribution to the lower mid position, where it would be close to the low *a*. At a later stage, *a* and ɔ merged in both long and short grades, for *a:* became ɔ: and ɔ became *a*. A new ɔ later arose from short *u*.

The Amarna form *nu-uḫ-ti* is exactly the way in which **nɔḥti* would have had to be written in Akkadian script.

The evidence of *me:t* 'he died' would seem to indicate a somewhat different development for the **e* perfects, for in closed syllables *a* is found as the reflex of **e*, e.g. *matta:* 'you (m.sg.) died'. In the light of the fact that many cases of West Semitic **i* have become *a* in Hebrew, this is not surprising, for any such change would almost inevitably have had to take place in two steps, one **i* → **e*, then **e* → *a*. And for the first step there is abundant evidence, since *e* so derived which was secondarily lengthened in an originally open syllable has remained, e.g. *ka:ḇe:ḏ* 'he was heavy' < **kabida*, but *ka:ḇadti:* 'I was heavy' < **kabidti*'. Therefore, the loss of the class is easy to understand, for after this change and the change of West Semitic **o:* and **o* to *a:* and *a*, the *e:* ~ *a* alternation would have become anomalous. What probably occurred then was gradual loss of the class as a distinct entity in the perfect, and merger of these forms with the II*w* perfects. This was a morphological re-patterning, not a phonological change, and is in full accordance with the natural development of the Hebrew language, where in each class of verbs one pattern has been gradually generalized.

Similar paradigmatic levelling may provide an answer to the alternation *o:* ~ *o* ~ ɔ found in three verbs in Hebrew, *ṭo:ḇ* 'he was good', *ʾo:r* 'it was light', and *bo:š* 'he was ashamed', where in closed syllables *o* and ɔ appear, e.g. *'bošta:* 'you (m.sg.) were ashamed', *bɔš'tɛm* 'you (m.pl.) were ashamed'. If one reconstructs for these forms, a rather peculiar fact manifests itself: since *o:* is derived from **a* and *o* ~ ɔ from **u*, **ba:θa* but **buθta* are the forms produced. And for the first form there is some support in the Ugaritic *'ar* 'it was light'.

Now, it is obvious that the reconstructions are identical to the largest class of Arabic II*w* perfects, and one could reasonably hypothesize that their origins are the same. But if this is so, how is one to explain the fact that in Hebrew this is found only in a tiny class of verbs, whereas in Arabic it occurs in the majority of hollow verbs? It is very difficult to accept that an irregular and relatively insignificant group could have taken over the regular verbs in the latter language—and only in the perfect moreover, not the imperfect, which would have had to remain untouched.

For this reason I hesitate to connect the two series of alternations to one proto-form. This hesitation is particularly valid in view of the fact that in terms of a synchronic grammar of Classical Hebrew, the alternation under discussion is not anomalous at all, and could be a result of regularization.

The Hebrew perfects show a three pattern system; the Arabic and Ethiopic show two patterns. Unless the Hebrew forms are to be called neologisms, and for this there is no evidence, then West Semitic must also have possessed three patterns, specifically **qo:ma*, **me:ta* and **ba:θa*, with short grades of these vowels in closed syllables. When *a:* became *o:*, then, an alternation would have been set up in the third class, e.g. **bo:θa* but **baθta*, which in terms of the language as it then existed was highly anomalous, since the verbs in which this occurred were relatively few and uncommon, and no other class of verbs had comparable alternation. At this stage, it should be remembered, **e* and **ɔ* had not yet become *a*, and therefore all other II*wy* perfects had in their closed syllables vowels which were merely the short grade of the long. Certainly, *e* < **i* is derived by a tone-placement which was different to that which produced **a:* → *o:* and must therefore have been later, and it is by merger with this *e* and later change of **e* to *a* that forms such as *matta:* were produced (cf. Harris (1939:50) with Kautsch (1910:47)). The next step, therefore, was the removal of the anomaly by the regularization of the verbs: the short grade of *o:* was levelled into the closed syllables of the perfects to produce **boθta* etc.

This is a possible explanation of the class. The only other explanation in terms of Hebrew alone would seem to be to derive them from triliteral forms, e.g. **tawuba*, **ʔawura* and **bawuθa* alongside the more general **qawama*, **bayana* and **mawita*. In this way it would be possible to attribute the different reflexes found to the different vowel in the second syllable. But if this is done, we will have fallen into a dangerous trap: in order to provide an answer for three irregular verbs, forms will have been produced for the regular verbs which could not have derived them, for reasons discussed above; moreover, some derived stems are inexplicable with such an origin (see below, Conclusion). In addition, these triliteral forms appear to be irreconcilable with the comparative evidence.

5. CONCLUSION

If the above argumentation is accepted, then it follows that late Classical Arabic, with its three vowel-phoneme system, cannot display the state of affairs which existed in West Semitic. The standard reconstruction of that system for the proto-language is therefore incorrect, and a system of five vowel-qualities must be proposed in its place. Whether the short grades of the mid vowels were phonemically distinct from the long remains to be discovered, but in the II*wy* perfects they were certainly allophones of the long. The Arabic changes **e* → *i* and **o* → *u* could not already have taken place at the time of the dissolution of West Semitic, for **i* and **u* have both merged in *ə* in Ethiopic, and **k'əmku* and **šəmku* would appear in this language rather than *k'omku* and *šemku*.[13]

[13]Note that it is possible that the vowel shortening constraint did not exist in the whole of West Semitic, but only in Central Semitic. If so, the Ethiopic forms are even easier to explain in that no merger of **e* with **e:* and **o* with **o:* is required, for forms such as **kʔo:mku* and **še:mku* would have existed. This does not, however, alter the fact that **e* and **o* could not have become *i:* and *u* respectively in W.S.

Restricted distribution may be part of the explanation for the loss of these vowels in Aramaic and Hebrew, but it should not be forgotten that in this latter case */e:/ never entirely disappeared but merely became less frequent for reasons earlier discussed. The loss of West Semitic */o:/ is, in the particular circumstances obtaining in Hebrew, not unexpected, for four-height vowel systems of the type hypothesized are peculiarly subject to change by merger, as the development of Romance and German shows.

The case of Arabic is much more clear. Once assimilatory *ʾimāla* and *tafkhīm* began to spread, generating *e:* and *o:* as allophones of *a:*, the West Semitic mid vowels were doomed. Among the first casualties was undoubtedly the Hijāzī dialect, for this must have lost the phonemes before *w* and *y* fell intervocalically, or the /e:/ and /o:/ found in the IIIwy verbs would also have disappeared. The cause for this is plain: *e:* and *o:* were in some positions allophones, in others phonemes. All that would be required for the loss of the latter would be for mid vowels to be reinterpreted as always allophonic, that is, always triggered by a surface segment. Since no such segment appears in III*wy* verbs, they became anomalous, and, to rectify the imbalance, *e:* and *o:* merged with *a:*, for this was the regular phone where no imalizing or tafkhimizing element was present.

This did not occur in the eastern Arabic dialects—upon which Classical Arabic was based (Rabin 1951:17-24) probably because of the early loss of intervocalic *w* and *y*, whereby a very large number of fresh cases of phonemic mid vowels took their place in the language, serving thereby as support for the old West Semitic mid vowels.

This early loss is substantiated by a comparison of pausal forms in the eastern and western dialects. Though by the time of the writings of the Arab grammarians these western dialects were being rapidly submerged, some of them still exhibited pausal forms ending in diphthongs, and contextual ending in pure vowels; for example the tribe of Fazāra and some of Qays[14] said *ʾafʿay* in the first case, and *ʾafʿa:* in the second, both meaning 'viper' (Sībawayhī 1975:4:181 standard ed. II:349). Given that the original form was **ʾafʿayu*, the development is easy to understand. Pausal forms in Arabic are produced primarily by deletion of final short vowels. If this rule had operated before the loss of intervocalic *w/y*, then the result would in fact be exactly the Fazāra forms. Since these are not found in Classical Arabic, the inference is obvious: it lost its semi-vowels before the rise of pausal forms, and Fazāra lost them afterwards.

The merger of the III*w* class of verbs into the III*y* further weakened the position of phonemic *e:* and *o:*. By the time of the classical language, the III*w* class had ceased to exist in the derived stems, and only in the G stem was the distinction maintained. At this stage every III*w* verb had a back mid vowel in its G stem and a front mid vowel in its derived stems. In this situation it is scarcely surprising that *ʾimāla* began to appear sporadically in the G stem as well.

But *e:* was also part of a more general process, which derived it as an allophone from *a:*. What is more, this *e:* alternated with *a:* in the same words, as the description of *ʾimāla* above has shown, for *e:* appeared before a following *y* or *i*. This means that the genitive in triptotes would have *e:* but the nominative and accusative would preserve *a:*, e.g. *kita:b{u/a}n* 'book'(nom./acc)but *kite:bin* (gen.). As long as the case vowels remained, this was a fairly automatic operation, but the moment they fell, as they did quite early, this automaticity was destroyed, and a very opaque series of structures was set up. The vowel *e:* could not even be taken as a marker of the genitive, for in the case of some members of the diptotic class, specifically the sound feminine plurals, it marked accusative

---

[14]Qays was a confederacy of both West and East Arabian tribes, so it is impossible to say which is referred to, but Fazāra was uncompromisingly West Arabian—it lived in the environs of the Ḥijāz.

as well. The vocabulary became arbitrarily divided into three classes: those where alternated with *e:*, those where *a:* never so alternated, and those where *e:* alternated with *o:*, all without surface conditioning factors.

The result of this confusion was inevitable. The phonemes *e:* and *o:* merged with *a:*, probably by the outright loss of *o:*, for it was in the weakest position, and the generalization of *a:* to all positions where pharyngeals and velar spirants were not adjacent. Indeed, in this we have an excellent explanation for the fronting of /a/ which is so evident in modern Arabic dialects.

The origin of these mid vowels is problematic. What is ideally required is comparative evidence of the stage immediately preceding the rise of mid vowels. And this is not likely to be found, although certainly more work needs to be done on Egyptian and the Berber dialects.[15] It is unlikely that Akkadian will be of value here, for it seems to display a situation which is closely analogous to the West Semitic. In addition, it has undergone far-reaching phonological change. It should nevertheless not be discarded without close investigation, particularly since its verbal morphology is significantly different to that of West Semitic, and the relationship of both systems to that of Proto-Semitic has up to this time been a field for speculative fantasy rather than sound linguistics, with a few exceptions, e.g. Kuryłowicz (1961, 1972).

In terms of the Semitic system as we know it now, it is not unreasonable to derive the West Semitic mid vowels ultimately from sequences of vowel and semi-vowel, e.g. **qawama* > **qo:ma*, **bayana* > **ba:na*, etc. This is even supported to some degree by the N stem, where both Hebrew and Arabic show reflexes which can only have come from *a:*, e.g. Arabic *inša:la* 'he was carried', *inšaltu* 'I was carried', Hebrew *na:qo:m* < **naqa:ma*, etc., and these differ from the G stem by having, in the regular verb, zero grade following the second radical. It is thus possible to derive them from forms such as **naqwama*, etc., and in favor of this is the fact that *w* and *y* directly following consonants are strangely rare in all Semitic languages of the more archaic type. But if this is so, how are the imperfects of the N stems to be derived? By the pattern of regular verbs, a II*wy* triradical imperfect would in theory have to be reconstructed as **yinqawimu*, etc., which should have yielded either **yiqqe:m* or **yiqqa:m* in Classical Hebrew but certainly not *yiqqo:m*, the form which is actually found. This is fact is a further argument against the existence of triliteral forms in Hebrew itself at an earlier date, for if **mawita* is to be the origin of Hebrew *me:ṯ*, then **yinqawimu* would certainly have produced **yiqqe:m*. In this case one could scarcely resort to analogy to explain the different vowel, for **yiqqe:m* would have been far closer to the regular Hebrew pattern, e.g. *yiqqa:ṭe:l*, than *yiqqo:m* is.

It is for reasons such as this that I feel that the derivation of the II*wy* verbs from triliteral forms must be treated with caution, though not totally rejected. There is no doubt that at some stage individual verbal forms did contain three surface radicals, particularly the Arabic perfect passive of the G stem, in which *i:* ~ *i* does not seem derivable from anything but *ü:* ~ *ü*, which in turn was derivable from **uwi* and **uyi*, e.g. **quwila* > *qü:la* > *qi:la* 'it was said'. These high front vowels still existed in some early Arabic dialects (Wright 1896:I:84) (one of which was probably Ḥijāzī, for they are used in Qur'anic recitation), and they can only be attributed to an allophonic assimilation of *u*

[15]Both of these display marked similarities to Semitic, yet are plainly not part of that grouping. The assertion that Egyptian is a result of language mixture between "Hamitic", i.e. non-Semitic Afroasiatic and Semitic, is based upon this fact. But a far more linguistically sound hypothesis is that Berber, Egyptian and Semitic are a subgroup: call it "North Afroasiatic", for want of a better name.

to a following *i* or *y*. There is no evidence for such a change in other Semitic languages, so it must have occurred internally to Arabic. In any event, the innovation clearly looks as if it took place at the same time and as part of the same process as assimilatory *ʾimāla* and *tafkhīm*.

Since, however, it is unlikely that this particular passive existed in Proto-Semitic (Kuryłowicz 1961:67-75), where the passive pattern was probably *faʿila*, all this proves is that, at the time of the origin of *fuʿila*, these verbs were interpreted as containing roots with middle radical semi-vowels, and it was on the basis of this that the new passives were formed.

REFERENCES

Bauer, H. and P. Leander. 1922. *Historische Grammatik der hebräischen Sprache*. Halle: M. Niemeyer.

Birkeland, H. 1940. *Akzent und Vokalismus in Althebräischen*. Oslo: Det Norske Videnskaps-Akademi.

Blake, F.R. 1942. "Studies in Semitic grammar II." *Journal of the American Oriental Society* 62:109-117.

Böhl, F.M.T. 1909. *Die Sprache der Amarnabriefe*. Leipzig: J.C. Hinrichs.

Cantineau, J. 1960. *Cours de Phonétique Arabe*. Paris: C. Klincksieck.

Caskel, J. 1968. *Liḥyan und Liḥyanisch*. Leyden: E.J. Brill.

Cowan, W. 1966. "Arabic evidence for Proto-Semitic */awa/ and */o/." *Language* 62:I:60-62.

Dillman, A. 1907. *Ethiopic Grammar*. Amsterdam: Philo.

Harding, G.L. 1952. *Some Thamudic Inscriptions from the Hashimite Kingdom of Jordon*. Leyden: E.J. Brill.

Harris, Z.S. 1939. *Development of the Canaanite Dialects*. New Haven: American Oriental Society.

Hetzron, R. 1974. "Extrinsic ordering in Classical Arabic." *Afroasiatic Linguistics* 1(3):1-20.

Howell, M.S. 1886. *A Grammar of the Classical Arabic Language*. Allahabad.

Ibn ʿAqīl. 1851. *Sharḥ ʾAlfiyyat Ibn Mālik*. Leipzig.

Jamme, A. 1967. *Thamudic Studies*. Washington.

Kautzsch, E. 1910. *Gesenius' Hebrew Grammar*. Oxford: OUP.

Kuryłowicz, J. 1961. *L'Apophonie en Sémitique*. Warsaw: Polska Akademia.

Kuryłowicz, J. 1972. *Studies in Semitic Grammar*. Warsaw: Polska Akademia.

Oxtoby, W.G. 1968. *Some Inscriptions of the Safaitic Bedouin*. New Haven: American Oriental Society.

Rabin, C. 1951. *Ancient West Arabian*. London: Taylor's Foreign Press.

Sībawayhī. 1977. *Kitāb*. Cairo: Al-hayʾat al-Misriyyat al-ʿĀmma li-l-Kitāb.

van den Branden, A. 1950. *Les Inscriptions Thamoudéennes*. Louvain: Bibliotheque de Muséon.

Winnett, F.V., and W.L. Reed. 1970. *Ancient Records from North Arabia.* Toronto: University of Toronto.

Wright, W. 1896-98. *Arabic Grammar,* 2 vols. Cambridge: CUP.

TITLES ON EBLA

Thoughts About Ibla: A Preliminary Evaluation, March 1977 By I. J. Gelb, *SMS* 1/1, 30pp., $3.20

A thorough and amply documented examination of the information presently available on the Ibla archives leads to new results in three major areas of interest. (1) With regard to *chronology*, palaeographic considerations require a dating of the texts to the period before Naram-Sim. (2) With regard to *cultural traditions*, important philological links may be established with Abu Salabikh, Mari and Kish: as a result a large non-Sumerian cultural area must be recognized already for the most ancient periods in the northern regions. (3) With regard to *linguistic affiliation*, a detailed analysis of the available material shows that Iblaic must be considered not as a dialect of West-Semitic, but rather as a new Semitic language, closer to Akkadian and Amorite than to Ugaritic or Hebrew.

Preliminary Remarks on the Royal Palace at Ebla By P. Matthiae, *SMS* 2/2, 22pp., 8 pls., $4.00

This article presents a preliminary picture of the 1973-1975 excavations of the Tell Mardikh Royal Palace G dating to Early Bronze IVA (ca. 2400-2250 B.C.). It was in 1975 that some 15,000 cuneiform tablets and fragments were found in the palace, some of them written in a new North-Western Semitic language. The various sectors of the palace thus far excavated are described and the building is placed within its chronological and historical framework. Ceramic evidence pertaining to the chronology is published here in detail for the first time. The paper (given here in a translation by Dr. Frances Pinnock) was read at the 24th Rencontre Assyriologique Internationale at Birmingham in July 1976.

Ebla in the Period of the Amorite Dynasties By P. Matthiae, *MANE* 1/6, 36pp., 20 pls., $6.50

This 1974 article on the archaeological documentation from Tell Mardikh came on the heels of the major discovery of the great archive of Ebla. As such, it provided the setting against which the discovery can best be appreciated, and it retains a classic value which makes its present English publication especially useful. Many new photographic illustrations add to the documentary value of the initial publication.

Old Canaanite Texts from Ebla By G. Pettinato, *MANE* 1/7, 17pp. $2.00

This article contains the first grammatical description of Eblaite, a new Semitic language attested in the texts from Tell Mardikh-Ebla. The article was first published in Italian in 1975 and is here published for the first time in English translation. It provides ample grammatical documentation from the first archive discovered in 1974 at Ebla, numbering 42 tablets. It also provides the first assessment of the linguistic and historical evidence of the texts.

AFROASIATIC LINGUISTICS

AAL includes contributions in linguistics within the vast domain of Afroasiatic (Hamito-Semitic) languages. Articles of general, theoretical interest using Afroasiatic material, descriptive, historical and comparative studies are included.

Volume One

Articles by P. Newman, R. G. Schuh, J. L. Malone, R. Hetzron, T. Givón, T. M. Johnstone, B. W. Andrzejewski, and H. Minkoff.

Volume Two

Articles by D. R. Cohen, C. D. Johnson, A. Barnea, R. Nir, C. T. Hodge, G. Janssens, S. Segert, J. B. Callender, J. L. Malone, T. Givón, and A. D. Corré.

Volume Three

Articles by R. G. Schuh, G. Buccellati, R. Hetzron, J. Saib, R. Steiner, D. Boyarin, I. Avinery, A. Zaborski, E. Rubinstein, and P. Abboud.

Volume Four

Issue 1: Neil Skinner, *North Bauchi Chadic Languages: Common Roots*, 49 pp.; and *'Fly' (Noun) and 'Mouth' in Afroasiatic*, 12 pp, $6.40.

Issue 2: Lewis Glinert, *Number Switch: A Singular Feature-change Rule in Modern Hebrew*, 38 pp., $4.00.

Issue 3: Russell G. Schuh, *Bade/Ngizim Determiner System*, 74 pp., $7.60.

Issue 4: Joshua Blau, *The Beginnings of the Arabic Diglossia. A Study of the Origins of Neoarabic*, 28 pp., $3.00.

Volume Five

Issue 1: Paul Newman, *Chadic Classification and Reconstructions*, 42 pp., $4.40.

Issue 2: D. L. Appleyard, *A Comparative Approach to the Amharic Lexicon*, 67 pp., $6.90.

Issue 3: Shmuel Bolozky, *Word Formation Strategies in the Hebrew Verb System: Denominative Verbs*, 26 pp., $2.80.

Issue 4: J. Rosenhouse, *On the Complexity of Some Types of Complex Sentences in Urban Moroccan Arabic and Some Other Arabic Dialects*, 15 pp., $1.70.

Issue 5: Janet H. Johnson, *Remarks on Egyptian Verbal Sentences*, 20 pp., $2.20.

Issue 6: Donald A. Burquest, *Semantic Parameters in Angas Kinship Terminology*, 29 pp., $3.10.

Volume Six

Issue 1: Malachi Barkai, *Theoretical Implications of Consonant Sequence Constraints in Israeli Hebrew*, 13 pp.; and Zev Bar-Lev, *The Ordering of Hebrew Morphological Processes*, 8 pp., $2.40.

Issue 2: Bernd Heine, *The Sam Languages: A History of Rendille, Boni and Somali*, 93 pp., $7.80.

Issue 3: Ruth Aronson Berman, *Lexical Decomposition and Lexical Unity in the Expression of Derived Verbal Categories in Modern Hebrew*, 26 pp., $2.80.

Issue 4: *Bibliographic Bulletin*, 17 pp., $2.00.

Issue 5: Ekkehard Wolff, *Grammatical Categories of Verb Stems and the Marking of Mood, Aktionsart, and Aspect in Chadic*, 48 pp., $5.00.

Issue 6: A.M.R. Aristar, *The IIwy Verbs and the Vowel System of Proto-West Semitic*, 17 pp., $2.00.

Volume Seven

Issue 1: Hans-Jürgen Sasse, *The Consonant Phonemes of Proto-East-Cushitic (PEC): A First Approximation*, 67 pp., $7.00.

Issue 2: Zafrira Malisdorf, *Love Through Death in Modern Hebrew. A Syntactic Treatment*, 16 pp., $1.80.

Issue 3: Francesco Antinucci an Annamaria Puglielli, *The Syntax of Indicator Particles in Somali: Relative Clause Construction*, 18 pp., $2.00.
